未完成

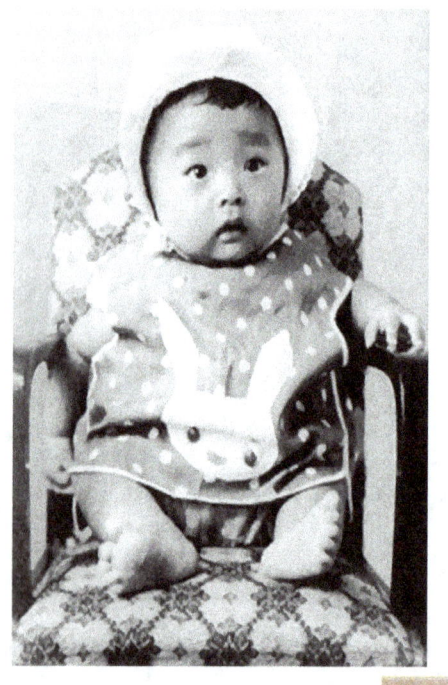

FUJICOLOR *HR* 85

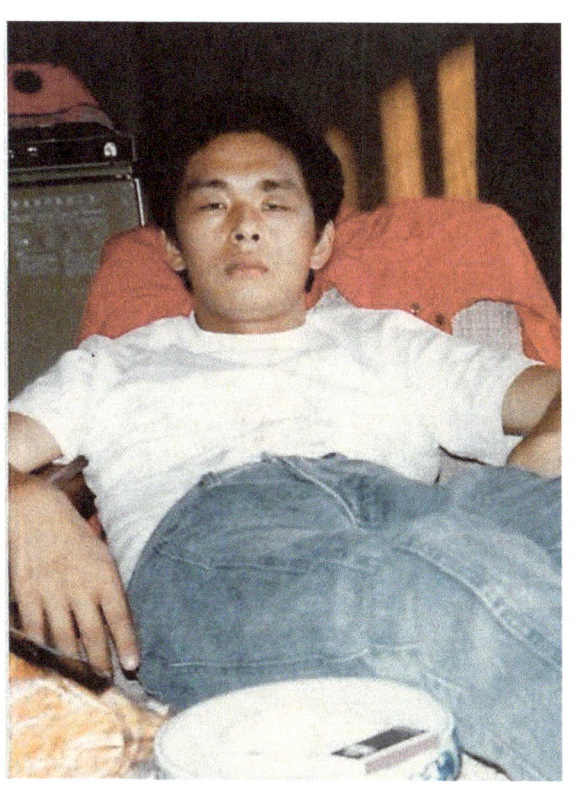

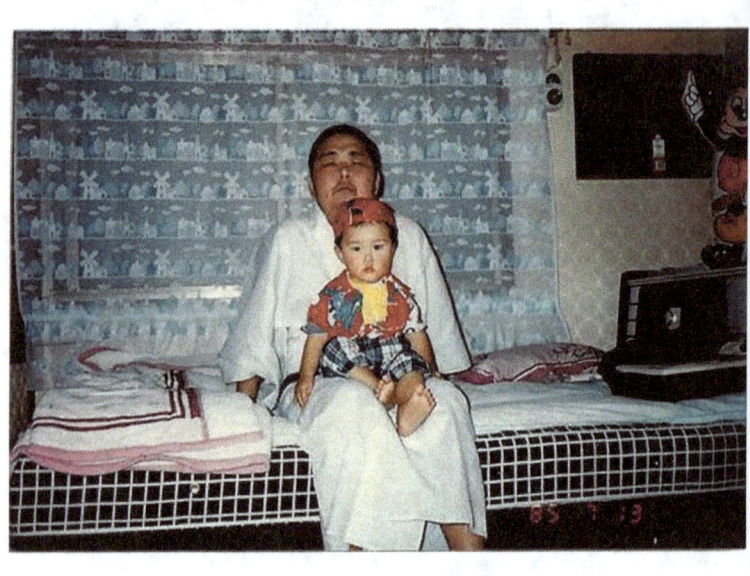

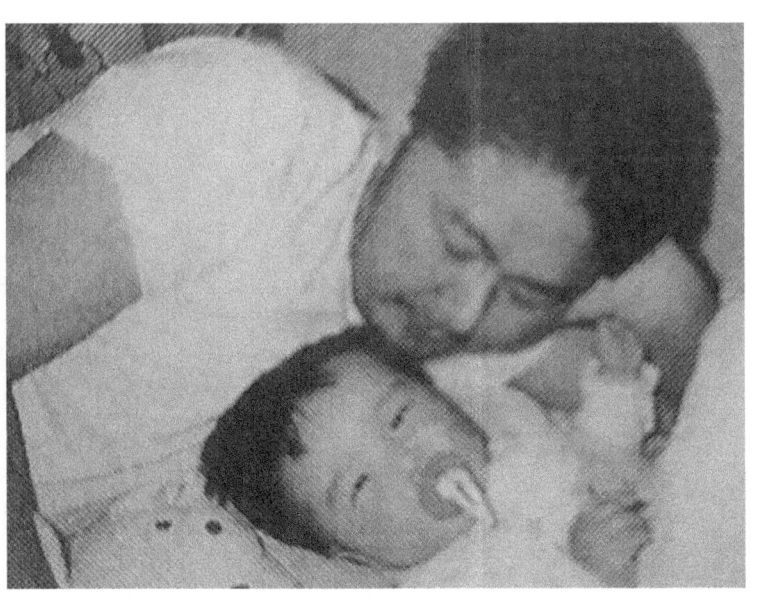

OTHER BOOKS BY ERIC HOFFMAN
PUBLISHED BY SPUYTEN DUYVIL

Daily Meditations by Philip Pain
This Thin Mean: New and Selected Poems
Losses of Life
Oppen: A Narrative
The Transparent Eye

住宅顕信
Sumitaku Kenshin

未完成
Mikansei
Unfinished

Translated by
Eric Hoffman

SPUYTEN DUYVIL
NEW YORK CITY

These haiku were published previously in *Otoliths*.

© 2023 Eric Hoffman
ISBN 978-1-959556-36-7
Cover art © 2023 Eric Hoffman
Cover design by t thilleman
Library of Congress Control Number: 2023012939

In memory of Kent Johnson, 1955–2022

BIOGRAPHICAL NOTE

Sumitaku Kenshin (住宅顕信, 1961—1987) was born Sumitaku Harumi (住宅春美) on March 21, 1961, in Okayama City, Okayama Prefecture. Initially intending to become a chef, in April 1976, Harumi entered Shimoda Gakuen Culinary School, from which he graduated in 1978. Around this time he began to read poetry, religion, and philosophy, and in September 1982, initiated his studies in Buddhism via a correspondence course through the Central Buddhism Academy (中央仏教学院). One year later, in July 1983, he became a priest of the Pure Land sect of Jodo Shinshu Hongwanji at the Nishi—Honganji (西本願寺) temple in Kyoto, where he was given the Buddhist name Saku Kenshin (roughly translated: "blossoming devotion"). That October, Kenshin married. The following February, he was diagnosed with acute myeloid leukemia and hospitalized at the Okayama Municipal Hospital. Upon learning of their new son-in-law's poor health, his wife's parents demanded a divorce, which she was awarded, but not before she she gave birth to Kenshin's child; a boy, Haruki, born in June 1984. Kenshin's parents took custody of Haruki yet, as Kenshin's younger sister Keiko worked in the Okayama Municipal Hospital, Haruki mostly lived with him in his hospital room. It was during this hospitalization that Kenshin discovered the work of Ozaki Hōsai and other New Trend haiku poets, including Nomura Shurindō, Taneda Santōka, Kaidō Hōko, Nakatsuka Ippekirō, and Ogiwara Seisensui. Kenshin became a member of the haiku group Sōun, studying under the tutelage of Sanikichi Ikeda. In 1985, Kenshin's improved health allowed him to leave the hospital, yet he soon suffered a relapse and had to be readmitted. Perhaps aware that he did not have long to live, in December, Kenshin self-published in clothbound hardcover his first collection, 試作帳 *Shisaku-chō*, here translated as *Experiment Book*, though previously rendered as *Prototype Book*, *Draft Book*, *Trial Pieces*, and *Experimental Notebook;* shisaku means trial manufacture, experiment, test piece, or prototype, though it can also mean the composition of a poem, and chō is a book, notebook, or album. In 1986, two of his poems were published in the journal *Sōun*, and another ninety in the free rhythm haiku journal *Kaishi*. Still others were published in *Umiichi*, of which he became a contributing editor. On February 7, 1987, just before his 26th birthday, Kenshin died of leukemia. His entire body of work, 281 haiku, were composed in the last twenty months of his life. His complete haiku, *Unfinished* (未完成 Mikansei), was published on February 7, 1988, the one year anniversary of his death.

C H R O N O L O G Y

1961 Born March 21st in Okayama City, Okayama Prefecture, the eldest son of Katsumoto (father) and Emiko (mother).

1966 Enters Okayama Municipal elementary school.

1973 Enters Okayama Municipal junior high school. Enjoys cartoons and plans a career in cartooning.

1976 Graduates from junior high school and enters Shimoda Gakuen Culinary School. Begins study of poetry, religion, and philosophy. Works at Okayama Kaikan. Starts love affair with Kawamoto Yokie, who is five years older than him.

1977 For 8 months, he and Yokie live together in his parent's house. Finds work at drive-in theater.

1978 Graduates from culinary school. Works at Tsudaka Grand Mart and Okayama Station Peach Plaza.

1980 Employed by Okayama City Hall Environment Business Office as a janitor. Begins to write haiku.

1981 Takes correspondence course at the Central Buddhism Academy.

1982 Graduates from the Academy in April.

1983 Ordained priest at the Nishi-Honganji Temple in Kyoto. Married in October. Visits Masaoka Shiki's and Taneda Santoka's monuments. Remodels part of parent's house to create altar for haiku poets he admires.

1984   Hospitalized on February 23rd due to leukemia. A son, Haruki, is born on June 14th. Divorces his wife. Parents assume custody of Haruki; Kenshin looks after Haruki in his hospital room. Begins to compose haiku and to study New Trend haiku. Studies under Sanikichi Ikeda. Reads works of Ozaki Hōsai.

1985   First haiku published in February issue of *Sôun*. Resigns from his position at Okayama City Hall. Collection 試作帳 *Shisaku-chō* published.

1986   Publishes haiku in *Sôun*, *Kaishi*, and *Umiichi*. Meets Takao Inoue and Asami Hashimoto. Temporarily discharged from hospital in April. Publishes newspaper article on free form haiku in Okayama Life newspaper. Forms "Okayama Jurokusha" group with Nishiyama Noriko and Matsumoto Hakuji and holds his first haiku meeting on May 11th. Visits the Okayama Living Shimbun with the woman who was his devoted attendant. On June 26th rehospitalized. In October, travels to Kyoto with his family.

1987   More haiku published in *Umiichi*. Dies February 7 at 11:23 p.m. at 25 years and 10 months old.

1988   *Mikansei*, a complete edition of his haiku is published by Yayoi Shobo, the same publisher as his prized *Collected Works of Ozaki Hōsai*, with a preface by Mikio Inoue.

1993   Monument of haiku 水滴のひとつひとつが笑っているだ is erected.

試作帳

Shisaku-chō

[Experiment Book]

Hospital room tedium
relieved by rain
at the window

Colder and colder,
the black telephone
in the night

Wakened by the sound of rain,
it continues to fall

My swollen face
in the mirror
I caress

White moon and an infusion bag
suspended in the night

In evening silence
I study the ceiling

My window faces
a distant mountain
cemetery

Through the ruins of a fire
muddy water flows

Window left open
to a clear blue sky

Mountain cemetery—
a tomb shines
in twilight

Hospital discharge postponed—
midday moon seen through the window

Evening IV reflects
a crooked moon

Night without sleep,
I rinse my face

Loneliness—
at night the black polish
of the telephone

My baby's sleeping face—
quietly I close the door

Hum of the fluorescent lamp—
I am engulfed by silence

Letter of resignation submitted,
another morning approaches my pillow

Evening window—
suddenly my face
appears

Bright voices of nurses
I see on their morning rounds

The day begins—
I remove the lid
from the thermometer

The nenbutsu in my mouth
turns into idle complaints

Having cried my heart out,
the look of relief
of my tear-stained face

Rain begins to fall—
the night's heartbeat

Inside the washbasin
my distorted face

Heavy, overcast sky—
not what I expected

Morning delayed
by rain that falls
outside the window

The same hands
clasped in prayer
swat the mosquitoes

Pondering the fact
that there is nothing to do—
evening deepens

Anemic,
another blood test
this morning

Needlework—
her warm hands
gently hold my own

This medicine
a lifetime companion,
this morning's medicine

My pulse measured,
all they've done
this tranquil morning

Even in dreams
my sister's apron
attends to my bedside

Cicada song—
I have not heard it
since I became ill

This summer
with this broken body,
somehow I manage to survive

I would like to walk the corridor
where the summer sun shines

On the table
a bottle of milk
glimmers in the morning sun

I walk amid morning dew
and visit a grave
in the autumn breeze

To give him thanks,
nenbutsu in the wind

Rain falls
and he cannot go out to play—
rubber boots

Naked body dried,
spied on by the moon

Neon brightness
excludes the light
of the moon

The day dawns slowly,
I walk up
to the window

Loneliness suggested
by the word processor's
clickclack tap of letters

In expectation of my return,
when I depart
I leave the door open

Work canceled by rain,
the town sleeps late

Typhoon's approach announced,
the radio shorts out

Cigarette stubbed out in the ashtray
with no intention to dispute

Weak from illness,
thin moon placed in the window

I am able to sit up—
daytime rain begins

I won't go against the tide—
I will walk as far as possible

Loneliness—
sadness ripples
in the pond

Home—cooked hot pot
eaten with chopsticks

Saké cup filled to the brim—
my face rejoices

At night the icy rain
curves on the window

My sick fingers shell
this hard—boiled egg

My shadow, too,
enjoys a poor side dish

Temperature taken—
the day begins,
the day ends

After the medical rounds,
not much else to do
but lie down in bed again

Ears against the pillow,
I still recognize the doctor's visit
by his footsteps

The rain's rhythm is steady—
autumn arrives at the hospital

Head pressed
into an ice pillow,
the day passes by

A difference of opinions—
one pillow on each bed

I want to run down the hall
like the wind that disturbs
the waiting room bulletins

Rain drizzle fogs the window—
I am anxious about tomorrow

Summer cloud—
a thought nearly forgotten
returns

I can only take a short walk
and let the morning sunshine in

Announcement of the extinguishing of the lamps
and then how bright the moon

Autumn has come—
the stethoscope is cold

No stars in the sky—
night's long curtains drawn

My little boy,
wanting to touch the stars,
raises high his hands

Sleepless,
night after night,
my pillow flipped over

My face
just one of many
in the elevator

The moon—
quietly the ice crumbles
in my ice pillow

I wake from anxious dreams
I do not remember

In front or behind
our shadows
keep pace with us

Flat cider
is my life

At play with the white clouds,
the blue sky is in good spirits

Winter comes,
opens the door that says
No Visitors

A distracted clam,
mouth left open,
closes it in a hurry

A lonesome dog
wags its tail
like a dog

The sick
reflected in the window
endure the winter sky

Again Orion
looks down at me—
winter night

Winter's long shadow
cast as I walk

A worm,
even crawling on the ground
I would want to live

In a puddle of water
the winter sky trembles

Bug stuck to the window—
winter has come

Always above my bed,
the black telephone rings

Bye-bye says my little boy,
palm of his hand,
back and front

Even in a world without death
there are so many tombs
for the soldier's ghosts

In contemplation,
my shadow walks with me

Milk not yet delivered,
rainy lazy morning

A cloud in my memory
becomes that face

One person's death
digitally read—
an icy expression

Without work to do
my fingers are lost
in thought

Lost at my window—
a cloud
without destination

Randoseru on the back,
its shadow arched
in the setting sun

In a black robe
I am an ordinary person
walking

I round the corner
to return,
moonlight on my back

From the steam of the bath,
one by one,
faces emerge

Tea refilled
fills me up

試作帳その後

Shisaku-chō Sonoato

[After That Draft Book]

I pass the time
with these books stacked
at my bedside

A new calendar hangs on the wall,
the start of a new year

Pale moonlight—
I walk a straight road

A cold hand takes my pulse—
my anxious thoughts turn
towards tomorrow

Stretched to the ends of the earth,
this lonesome shadow

In the operation waiting room
the minute hand chases
the hour hand

Always sick,
I am at least able
to draw the curtains

A moment without pain,
pale moon in daylight

Evening wind
like Morse code
howls out an SOS

Late at night
the IV breathes
quietly

It is winter again
even in the frozen words
of the visitors

The cloud forms a face
anticipated since morning

Winter's law—
Orion at his proper station
in the window

I rise—
the starry sky wavers

Allowed to go outside,
I walk toward the moon,
vague in daylight

A discarded doll,
its mechanisms revealed

Curled up,
my dreams concealed
for tomorrow

Fallen ill,
my friends diminish—
I write New Year's cards

New desk calendar
for the new year
leans against my pillow

Robot grasped tightly—
he smiles in my dream

Year's end—
both legs cleansed

Medicine by my bedside,
I celebrate the new year

Only the TV wishes me
a Happy New Year

A peaceful day—
the correct selection of music
for a winter day

My hearing lost,
the silent infinity
of a blue sky

Morning sun illuminates
the surgery consent letter's red seal

Our thin bodies
stand in line
for the morning weigh-in

Name called,
I open the heavy door
to the examination room

A sheet of paper
at my bedside
announces the operation

Clock ticks, I find myself
at the operating room entrance

Drowsy from anesthesia,
pale midday moon
at the window

At night
my square of sky
is filled with stars

Jingle Bells played in quick rhythm—
in this city the year comes to an end

The moon distorted
by a high fever

A girlfriend gone to bed—
the moon wanes

Am I an oni?
The beans thrown at me

When will spring arrive?
the cherry blossoms
already in my heart

Even from the depths of my wheelchair,
springtime finds a line in my sight

I rub my legs—
walk in sunlight

My face reflected in the window—
no sign of spring

Deep breath
into thin lungs—
cold x-ray

Cold x-ray in early spring
pressed against my chest

Exposed by x-rays,
my solitary heart

On the IV bottle
cherry blossoms
already scattered

A desire for suicide
burns deep in my heart

Youth
is like this
lonely spring

In the sun
my shadow
weak and faded

Two windows on a hill
look down into the night

Eyes opened,
discomforting things seen—
eyes closed

Freezing rain falls—
they say that spring approaches

My child is old enough
to say bye—bye
on the telephone

EKG—
I hear my heartbeat
alone

Cold morning—
only the backs of lonely people
walking away

The door opens
and a familiar voice
calls out to me

Immersed in conversation
the stars become more visible

Head shaven—
I feel the heat
of the sun

Happiness—
submerged in a hot bath
overflowing

Each drop of water
has a smiling face

A smiling face floats
in the flow of hot water

The traffic signals flash off and on
like the pulse of the night

Spring breeze—
the front gate is heavy

All day a headache
from the infusion

Alone in the gloom
of my hospital room,
the sound of rainfall

The rain falls
all day long
outside my window

Head hung low,
I walk the streets
absent my shadow

My body unable to do anything
other than be disobedient
to my parents

I look up
at the wide sky
there before me

Under a thin sun
men and sparrows
warm themselves

A life of poverty—
rain strikes
the tin roof

Allowed a shower,
a morning rainbow appears

This thin body
is my only one—
I wash it thoroughly

Lonesome father and son
look up at the lonely stars

Even from a distance
I recognize
your white blouse

In my deaf ear
I am told of the death
of a friend

Sickness makes me stagger—
the ants at my feet
go to work

From this hill I've climbed
summer approaches

You can cry out for mommy
yet you have no mother,
little boy

I walk and walk and yet
my shadow precedes me

A drunken moon
hangs from the sky

Early spring—
on a grand scale
a grasshopper leaps

In the faint shadow
of her parasol
I fall in love

Summit reached—
the sky leads me
to summer clouds

Mountain charm
whittled away
by summer

The conversation wanders—
hands in my pockets

Face washed—
I cannot show myself
to my son

Black cemetery wreath—
callous sky

Night falls swiftly
on the faces
of the funeral procession

Returned home late at night,
umbrella folded up

Nobody here—
I sit next to the wall

I cling tight
to the evening—
cough and cough

We meet again—
I look at you
with the moon so thin

It is cold and rainy—
I lie upon a stretcher

I fall ill—
seen from my sickbed
a swallow flies low

Confronted with sadness—
I pick up my chopsticks

A slight shadow
argues with another

All alone
I light up the room
brilliantly

My hearing lost,
the birds are still
reputed to sing

The ceiling's silence
conveys the depth of night

Tired of waiting,
the umbrella stands
upright

The IV drip hangs heavy—
I place my order
for today's dinner

The postbox mouth is open—
streets are wet with rain

With loneliness
a swing creaks
after the rain

Propped up on an ice pillow—
the ceiling is always there

Blood from my lungs
held up to the light
of a cloudy sky

Dead of night—
thin needle
searches for a vein

For each person a window,
for each person a moon—
such loneliness

Too weak to lift up my son,
I crouch down next to him

This morning—
imprisoned in the shadows
of the blinds

I run to the window—
morning bed sheets changed

Light as a breeze
I step upon the scale

It grows dark—
I see him off,
watch him walk away

Head entrusted
to the autumn wind,
I shave

In firework light
I find my shadow
on the road

My shadow separate
from the mass of shadows

After a bath
I wipe dry
my deaf ear

Humid room—
I kill an ant
and another appears

Invalid gloom—
the rain begins to fall

I massage my face
with a solitary hand

Even my son
calls me deaf

Crouched beside a pool of water
we look like a father and son

Temperature rises,
so too the road

Nothing in my pockets
but my hands

My lonesome
fingernails grow

The sun is out—
the hospital looks crooked

In the mirror
I force my palsied face
to smile

It cannot be helped—
the medicine swallowed deeply

Alone—
only the sounds of loneliness
surround me

Cigarette crushed
along with every word

We begin to talk
then reach a conclusion—
cigarette reduced to ashes

The wind blows
down a straight road—
the moon ascends

A dragonfly,
thin wings
sick in summer

My silent wife
makes me nervous—
summer heat

A cold spoon
for thin rice gruel
placed beside my pillow

Freezing rain falls—
I speak on the telephone

Heavy cloud on my back—
there is nowhere
for me to go

Hearing aid placed in my ear,
I hear the birds chirp

Rainy day—
the door creaks—
alone in this hospital room

In the depth of night
I hit the mosquito
then hear it buzz

Rain falls,
calms my mind

Mosquitoes buzz
in my hearing aid—
I shut it off

Bad dream—
I wake with sweaty palms

Springtime approaches—
snow on the road
begins to melt

Rainclouds—
sadness and bitterness
begins to fall

Casually imitating his father,
my son bites his nails

Window wiped,
I can see the city—
cold morning

Stone mountain quarried—
autumn approaches

Leaving the hospital room,
I breathe the autumn mountain air

Lined up against the blue sky,
cold graves made from stone
stand guard

Morning moonlight
on the cold windowsill—
I touch it

I make my way through
a crowd of people
then warm my hands

Autumn descends
from the deep mountains

In moonlight
my cough is blue

Lonely autumn,
bit by a mosquito

In moonlight
a cold shadow sings

The moon lingers
in the morning sky—
I ponder yesterday

A cold blue sky
as far as I can see

Evening glow—
I search for the face
of my child

The moon rests
behind my desk—
the night is long

An unbearable sensation—
knife slices an apple

The sound of the rain
falls deeply
into the evening pond

Shadow on shōji—
a lonely cough

Crematory smokestack
seen on a winter mountain

Cold night—
already freezing,
the wallpaper peels off

Cold moon reflects
in the water of the dipper—
I rinse out my mouth

Chilly morning—
we wait in line
to be weighed

Allowed a bath,
I pop soap bubbles

Swift as wind
he races down
the corridor

Rain at any minute,
even the chopsticks are heavy

The moon sheds
a chilly sound

Hurried by the extinguishing of the lights,
my little son waves goodbye

His shoulders wet with rain,
my son nestles close to me

The moon affixed
to a closed window

The sound of water—
winter approaches

Been away from home
for a very long time—
look up at the moon

A soaking wet puppy

Nenbutsu—
my breath is cold white

Winter arrives,
stubbornly wants
to shut me in

Head turned,
I see my shadow
in the moonlight

The rain buries the air
in ginkgo leaves,
sticky with water

The night is sad—
someone begins to laugh

Eric Hoffman is the author of several books of poetry, most recently *Circumference of the Sun* (Dos Madres Press, 2021). He lives in Connecticut.

www.ingramcontent.com/pod-product-compliance
Lightning Source LLC
Chambersburg PA
CBHW071013120626
46546CB00003B/1070

* 9 7 8 1 9 5 9 5 5 6 3 6 7 *